KIDS FIGHT PLASTIC

MARTIN DOREY

ILLUSTRATED BY TIM WESSON

WALKER
BOOKS

D0177135

CONTENTS

ARE YOU READY TO BE A SUPERHERO?

HOW TO BE A #2MINUTESUPERHERO

Have you got 2 minutes?
2 minutes is all the time it takes
to become a superhero.
Not all superheroes fly
or save the world from alien invaders.
Some superheroes do simple,
everyday things, that only take
a couple of minutes and add
up to make a huge difference.
These superheroes are just
like you and me. They live
among us, in secret,
doing amazing things.
You can be one too.

WE NEED SUPERHEROES TO SAVE THE OCEAN

You are probably wondering why we need superheroes. It's simple. We need superheroes to **FIGHT PLASTIC** and **SAVE THE OCEAN**.

Our oceans are dying because we are using them as a dump, allowing them to fill with plastic. Our plastic rubbish is hurting the creatures that live in or around the ocean. If we don't watch out, plastic rubbish will hurt us too.

WE NEED SUPERHEROES LIKE YOU

Everything you do – good or bad – has an effect on the world around you. **FIGHTING PLASTIC** is a brilliant way you can change the world for the better.

Doing something simple for 2 minutes every day – such as picking up plastic litter – turns you into a superhero. Every small thing you do to fight plastic helps save the ocean. It also makes people around you take notice.

Politicians and big companies might say they care about fighting plastic, but in my experience they spend ages taking action, if they do anything at all.

So why wait?

YOU CAN FIGHT PLASTIC RIGHT NOW BY BECOMING A #2MINUTESUPERHERO.

WHY WE MUST FIGHT PLASTIC FOR THE OCEAN

- Over 8 million tonnes of plastic enter the ocean each year.

- Every square mile of ocean has 46,000 items of plastic in it.

- Plastic is now present in every part of the ocean, including the Arctic sea ice and at the bottom of the Mariana Trench, the deepest part of the world's oceans.

- It is estimated that by 2050 there will be more plastic (by mass) than fish in the ocean.

- Plastic does not biodegrade (break down into natural materials). All it does is break down into smaller and smaller pieces, known as microplastics.

- As plastic breaks down, it releases harmful chemicals that are believed to be contributing to climate change: the gradual warming of the planet due to human activity.

The oceans are vital to all of us, no matter where we live.

The oceans regulate our weather and make the air cleaner. They also provide us with half of the oxygen we need to breathe to stay alive. And they absorb carbon dioxide, a gas that contributes to climate change and global warming.

The oceans provide food. Around 90 million tonnes of fish are caught each year. Without this source of food many people would starve.

The oceans are home to whales, dolphins, turtles, otters, seals, fish, sharks, rays, plankton, manatees, lobsters, crabs and jellyfish, as well as seaweeds, grasses and algae.

The oceans are a fantastic, vast and wonderful playground for swimming, snorkelling, splashing and surfing!

We have to look after them.

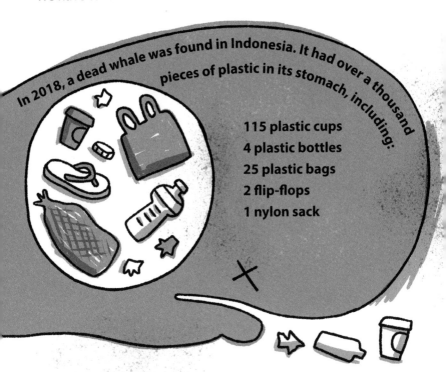

In 2018, a dead whale was found in Indonesia. It had over a thousand pieces of plastic in its stomach, including:

115 plastic cups
4 plastic bottles
25 plastic bags
2 flip-flops
1 nylon sack

WHY WE MUST FIGHT PLASTIC FOR WILDLIFE

- Plastic entangles sea creatures: estimates suggest 100,000 sea mammals – whales, dolphins and turtles – and 1 million seabirds die each year because of plastic entanglement or ingestion.

- Lost plastic fishing gear entangles and kills thousands of fish and animals each year.

- Tiny organisms, called algae, grow on plastic in seawater. The algae give off chemicals which mean the seabirds mistake the plastic for food. Seabirds that eat plastic die hungry, unable to digest it. Chicks with stomachs full of plastic can't fledge (learn to fly) so are stuck on the water.

- Fish mistake tiny bits of plastic for food, eat them and starve. If we eat fish there is also the chance that we could end up eating the plastic the fish have eaten.

- Plastic attracts Persistent Organic Pollutants (POPs) in seawater. These chemicals build up on plastic, becoming more and more toxic. The POPs can then bio-accumulate up the food chain. This means that if a big fish eats a little fish, it absorbs the toxins. Then when that fish gets eaten by a bigger fish, the toxins pass on to that fish! In theory, these toxic chemicals could enter the human food chain.

EVERYDAY SUPERHERO

Name: Captain Flipper

Job: Seal

Superpower: Stays underwater for up to 30 minutes

How you fight plastic: I survived getting tangled in 9 metres of net

Top tip: Every bit of plastic you pick up can help an animal

Hates: Plastic in the sea

Loves: Being rescued by the Cornish Seal Sanctuary

CAPTAIN FLIPPER

MEET THE EVERYDAY SUPERHEROES

But don't despair! Superheroes live among us. They don't have flashy costumes or their own TV shows. Lots of them fight plastic because they believe it's the right thing to do. Some, like Captain Flipper, are superheroes because they fight plastic to survive. You're going to meet some more everyday superheroes in this book. I hope they inspire you to become a superhero too.

MARTIN AND HIS #2MINUTE MISSION

Let me tell you a bit about me. My name is Martin and I'm going to train you to become a **#2minutesuperhero**. I hate waste, particularly plastic waste, and think there are lots of ways we can fight plastic in our lives.

I live in a town on the coast. It's like any other town, except it has a beach. Rubbish washes up onto the beach with every tide. After storms it can be heartbreaking. I go and pick it up, but I know that there will always be more. So I need help.

The more you fight plastic, the more you help the ocean, my beach and beaches all over the world. Wherever you live, you are connected to the ocean by rivers, waterways, sewers and drains. If we stop plastic getting into the water, we stop it washing up on the beach.

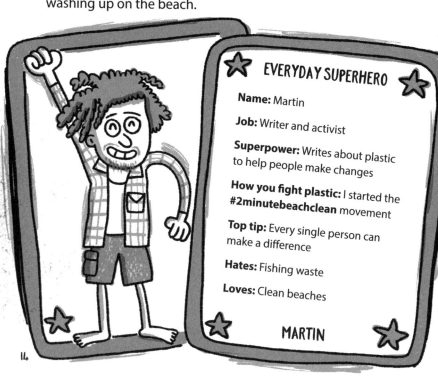

⭐ EVERYDAY SUPERHERO ⭐

Name: Martin

Job: Writer and activist

Superpower: Writes about plastic to help people make changes

How you fight plastic: I started the **#2minutebeachclean** movement

Top tip: Every single person can make a difference

Hates: Fishing waste

Loves: Clean beaches

MARTIN

THE #2MINUTEBEACHCLEAN

In 2013, I decided to do something about the rubbish on my beach. I quickly picked up some rubbish and took a picture of it. I posted my picture online using a brand-new hashtag, **#2minutebeachclean**, hoping someone might see it and take 2 minutes to do the same thing.

Amazingly, they did. By spring 2019, there were over 120,000 pictures of people picking up litter posted on Instagram from all over the world.

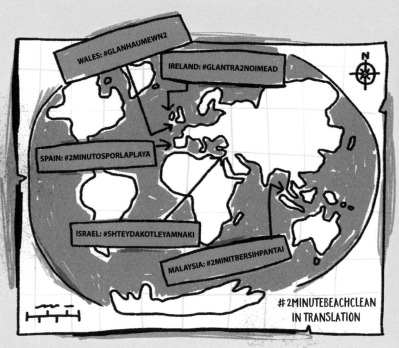

WALES: #GLANHAUMEWN2

IRELAND: #GLANTRA2NOIMEAD

SPAIN: #2MINUTOSPORLAPLAYA

ISRAEL: #SHTEYDAKOTLEYAMNAKI

MALAYSIA: #2MINITBERSIHPANTAI

#2MINUTEBEACHCLEAN IN TRANSLATION

ANALYTIC PLASTIC: It is estimated that each **#2minutebeachclean** weighs 2 kilograms, which means that 240 tonnes of litter have been picked up since 2013 – at least!

HOW TO USE THIS BOOK

- This book is separated into **MISSIONS**, which are all about the areas of your life where you can fight plastic, ways to do it and why it's important.

- In each mission you'll also find a series of **2 MINUTE MISSIONS**. These are tasks that I want you to complete. Each of them is worth **SUPERHERO POINTS**.

- Some missions are hard, but will earn you more points. You might need an adult to help. Some missions are easy!

- As you complete each mission, make a note of how many points you have scored.

- Once you have got to the end of the book – and the end of your superhero training – you will be able to work out your final score. This will give you a **SUPERHERO RATING**.

What kind of **#2minutesuperhero** will you be?

SUPERHERO STAT: 9 out of 10 superheroes don't even know they are superheroes yet.

READY FOR ACTION?

Before you begin your first mission, I need you to make this promise.

I solemnly swear to pledge my allegiance to the ocean.

I will take care of the oceans through my everyday actions and will use **2** minutes of each day to fight plastic.

Training approved by:

Founder of the #2minutebeachclean

THE #2MINUTESUPERHERO RULES

Fighting plastic isn't impossible. You can do it. But at some point or other you are going to have to pick up someone else's litter. It's horrible, but it must be done! To keep you safe, here are some rules you have to follow.

YOUR MISSIONS START NOW...

GET TO KNOW THE BAD STUFF

Let's start your training by learning about the bad stuff. Your first mission is to get to know about plastic and, in particular, single-use plastic. That's the plastic that gets used just once and then thrown away. That's the bad stuff we want to fight. The good stuff, on the other hand, makes toys, gadgets and life-saving medical equipment, and is used for long periods of time.

THE HISTORY OF PLASTIC

Plastic – in some form or other – has been around for a long time. It can be moulded or shaped, making it an incredibly useful material for all kinds of things, from computers and cables to toys and medical equipment.

The first plastic to be made from oil was invented about one hundred years ago. It was called Bakelite, and you can still find it in old houses (look for brown light switches). Since then our world has become more and more reliant on oil-based plastic.

Over the last hundred years, different types of plastic have been invented for all kinds of uses: Perspex is clear and replaces glass for windows. Polypropylene makes syringes for injections. High-density polyethylene makes plastic bags and milk bottles. Nylon makes clothes, carpets and nets.

IDENTIFYING PLASTICS

Most plastic items you buy new will have a symbol on them which says what type of plastic the item is made from. Different plastics have different properties. Some plastics float in water; others don't. Some can be recycled, while others can't. Some are more toxic than others.

CODE AND SYMBOL	PLASTIC TYPE	TYPICALLY USED FOR	PROPERTIES
01 PET	Polyethylene terephthalate	Soft drink bottles, food trays	RECYCLABLE Clear, tough, sinks
02 PE-HD	High-density polyethylene	Yogurt containers, shopping bags, milk bottles, shampoo, detergent bottles	RECYCLABLE Floats in water
03 PVC	Polyvinyl chloride	Blister packs, pipes and hoses, clear food packaging	RECYCLABLE Considered to be the most toxic of all plastics
04 PE-LD	Low-density polyethylene	Rubbish bags, squeezable bottles, cling film	RECYCLABLE Floats in water
05 PP	Polypropylene	Bottle caps, straws, food tubs	RECYCLABLE Floats in water
06 PS 06 PS-E	Polystyrene, expanded polystyrene	Plastic cutlery, CD cases, cups, plates	NOT EASY TO RECYCLE Releases chemicals that are believed to cause cancer
07 OTHER	Polycarbonate resins and composite material	Components, computers, electronics, nylon, Perspex	NOT EASY TO RECYCLE Any plastics that can't be categorized by the other 6. Toxic.

WHEN PLASTIC IS GOOD

Plastic is fantastic. It is light, strong and cheap, which means lots of things are made from it. Toys, such as Lego, Star Wars figures, dolls and Xboxes are all made from plastic.

It's durable too, so it doesn't rust or decay like metal or wood. It will last in some form for hundreds of years, which makes it a practical choice of material. Plastic can also be reused many times. Some types are recyclable.

Medical equipment is often made from plastic. In fact, some advances in medicine wouldn't have happened without plastic. Lots of people who need disability aids, medicines or medical equipment rely on plastic to live better lives.

SURPRISING PLASTICS

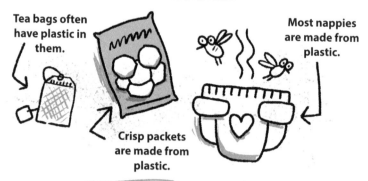

Tea bags often have plastic in them.

Most nappies are made from plastic.

Crisp packets are made from plastic.

YOUR 2 MINUTE MISSION: Find five pieces of good plastic that you use every day.
10 POINTS

WHEN PLASTIC IS BAD

One of the problems with plastic is that it is made from oil, which takes millions of years to form.

Oil is a non-renewable resource, so once we've used it all up, it's gone and we can't make more of it. The other problem is that plastic is durable. It doesn't biodegrade like wood or rust away into non-toxic materials. It is PERSISTENT and unless we do something with it, plastic will never go away. If it does break down – because it's been in the sea or in the ground – it just breaks down into smaller and smaller pieces. It also releases chemicals that are bad for the planet in the process.

Plastic has become one of the most-used materials on the planet, but we haven't yet worked out what to do when we've finished with it! Doh!

We allow it to persist in the environment by letting it flow into the sea or burying it in landfill. So maybe it's not plastic that's bad. Maybe it's the way we use plastic in our daily lives – without thinking about it – that's the problem.

YOUR 2 MINUTE MISSION: **Find five pieces of bad plastic that will only be used once before being thrown away. 20 POINTS**

THE HISTORY OF PLASTIC

1907
The first synthetic plastic to be made from oil – Bakelite – is created.

1930
Sticky tape is invented.

2004
The term microplastics is first used to describe tiny plastic particles that pollute the environment.

1976
Plastic becomes one of the most-used materials in the world.

2009
The Boeing 787 aeroplane is made from 50% plastic.

2015
Oceanographer films a turtle with a straw up its nose.

2017
Blue Planet II opens the world's eyes to the problem of plastic.

1941

The first polyester fibre, Terylene, is kept secret because of World War 2.

1949

The first plastic Airfix models are built.

1958

Plastic Lego bricks are invented.

1969

Neil Armstrong plants a nylon flag on the moon.

⭐ EVERYDAY SUPERHERO ⭐

Name: Rob

Job: Underwater rubbish collector

Superpower: Transforms plastic fishing nets into kayaks

How you fight plastic: I run a diving group that collects plastic on the seabed

Top tip: Shout about plastic pollution

Hates: People who think single-use plastic is OK

Loves: Turning old plastic into something useful

ROB

FIGHT PLASTIC IN YOUR BIN

I love talking rubbish. But not because I like seeing it! It's because I like working out what I should do with it. If you're going to fight plastic – and become a #2minutesuperhero – you're going to have to get to know your bin!

WHAT'S IN OUR WASTE?

- The UK produces around 222.9 million tonnes of household waste each year.

- The average person in the UK produces around 600 kilograms of waste per year.

- On average, around 45% of that waste gets recycled.

- Plastic makes up around 44% of all UK recycling.

- 11.5 million tonnes of packaging waste is produced in the UK each year.

WHAT HAPPENS TO YOUR WASTE?

You put things in the bin and then forget about them. Off they go and that's that. Sadly, it's not. Everything has to go somewhere. But where? There is no "away" to throw stuff into. We need to think carefully about what happens to the waste in our household bin.

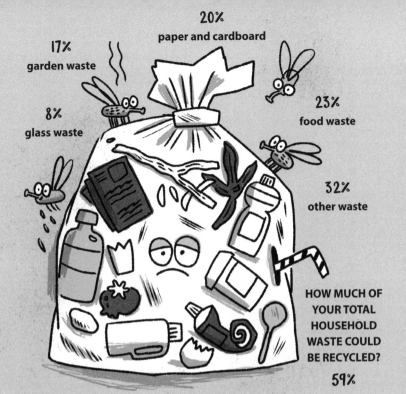

20%
paper and cardboard

17%
garden waste

8%
glass waste

23%
food waste

32%
other waste

HOW MUCH OF
YOUR TOTAL
HOUSEHOLD
WASTE COULD
BE RECYCLED?
59%

WHAT HAPPENS TO FOOD AND GARDEN WASTE?

Food and garden waste is organic matter and can be put into
a home compost bin. It will break down into a concoction
of natural materials, known as compost, that will benefit the
planet and help new life to grow. Amazing!

Waste that is certified as home compostable, like some
magazine wraps and some types of food bin bags, can also
be put in your home compost. Some councils collect
food and garden waste for composting.

YOUR 2 MINUTE MISSION: **Get a food waste bin and start
a compost heap! Find out how to make compost in
Mission 8.**
30 POINTS

WHAT HAPPENS TO YOUR HOUSEHOLD WASTE?

If you put stuff in your recycling bin, it will go to:

- a MRF (Materials Recovery Facility, pronounced "MuRF"), where it is sorted into recyclable and non-recyclable waste.

If you put stuff in your household waste bin, it will either go to:

- landfill, a hole in the ground, where it may leak chemicals and greenhouse gases (the gases that contribute to global warming and climate change). Not good!

- energy recovery, which is when waste is burned to make electricity. It's good that waste is turned into useful energy, but bad because it could be recycled.

WHAT HAPPENS TO YOUR RECYCLABLE WASTE?

Recyclable waste – which you sort into your recycling bin – is collected and turned into something else. Or so you thought!

It's silly, but recycling doesn't always get recycled. It all depends on the quality of recycling (how clean it is), the type of materials (some plastics are worth more than others) and the value of each material on the open market.

Basically, some recycling gets recycled. Some doesn't.

Confusing? Yup. While recycling is VITAL, it is not always the best way to fight plastic.

The best way? Say no to single-use plastic. Reuse stuff. Reduce the amount of stuff you have. Repair your stuff!

RECYCLING THE FACTS: Until 2017, the UK shipped a lot of recycling to China. Now China no longer takes it, which means it has to go somewhere else. It may end up in landfill or the ocean.

WHAT ABOUT BIODEGRADABLE AND COMPOSTABLE PLASTICS?

Sorry! If only it was as simple as recyclable and non-recyclable.

If something is labelled compostable, it will break down – like food waste. But often compostable packaging will only break down under certain conditions in industrial composters, at the right temperature, at a council facility. Another problem is that compostable waste can spoil recycling, so it is difficult to know what to do with it.

Biodegradable items, such as straws and cutlery, will break down eventually into organic matter, but often this has to happen under controlled conditions in a special facility.

New plastics, or bioplastics, are being developed from anything from sugar cane to soya. The great thing about them is that they aren't made from oil and don't leave nasty chemicals when they degrade. The downside is that unless they are disposed of properly, they can be as persistent as normal plastic.

I know! My head is about to explode too.

YOUR 2 MINUTE MISSION: **Find three straws – one that is plastic, one that is biodegradable plastic and one that is paper. Get a plant pot and fill it with mud. Then poke the straws halfway into the mud. Leave them for a couple of weeks and see what happens!**
20 POINTS

WHAT HAPPENS TO WASTE IN OTHER COUNTRIES?

In some countries, where they don't have recycling plants or refuse collections, rubbish gets put in dumps and burned, thrown in rivers where it ends up in the sea, or just left to rot (or not, if it's plastic). And littering is a problem across the world. Many countries and cities are trying to stop rubbish piling up in the streets and fields by taking steps to ban single-use plastic. Hurrah!

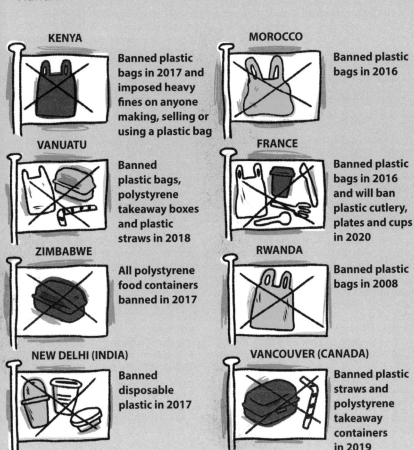

KENYA
Banned plastic bags in 2017 and imposed heavy fines on anyone making, selling or using a plastic bag

MOROCCO
Banned plastic bags in 2016

VANUATU
Banned plastic bags, polystyrene takeaway boxes and plastic straws in 2018

FRANCE
Banned plastic bags in 2016 and will ban plastic cutlery, plates and cups in 2020

ZIMBABWE
All polystyrene food containers banned in 2017

RWANDA
Banned plastic bags in 2008

NEW DELHI (INDIA)
Banned disposable plastic in 2017

VANCOUVER (CANADA)
Banned plastic straws and polystyrene takeaway containers in 2019

FIGHT PLASTIC IN YOUR PARK

How often do you go to the park? Do you ever see litter? What about that plastic bottle you see out of the corner of your eye when you fly down the slide? You know the one!

Do you ever imagine that a piece of litter, left in your park or street, could find its way to the sea? It can! All plastic in the ocean comes from somewhere – and you don't want it to come from your park. Right? This is why your BIG fight against plastic starts right here, right now, in your street, park or school playground.

YOUR 2 MINUTE MISSION: Do a #2minutelitterpick.
On your walk home from school or at the park,
spend 2 minutes filling an old carrier bag with litter.
Recycle what you can and bin the rest. How much
did you get in 2 minutes?
20 POINTS

HOW THE PLASTIC IN YOUR PARK GETS IN THE OCEAN

Believe it or not, your park, street or playground is connected to the ocean. All drains lead to sewage works, watercourses or rivers that, in turn, lead to the sea.

The rubbish that your family – and all the other families on your street – puts out every week also has a route to the ocean. If your bin bags burst open or your wheelie bin blows over and spills plastic in your street, it can be blown into a drain or river and then be carried out to sea. The same happens with litter.

If you keep your street, playground or park plastic-free, then you'll be helping to look after the ocean.

That's why YOU are important in the fight against plastic.

EVERYDAY SUPERHERO

Name: Neil

Job: Litter-picker

Superpower: Keeps the country tidy

How you fight plastic: I pick up litter anywhere and everywhere I can

Top tip: Stay positive. We can do this!

Hates: People who watch you pick up litter but don't get stuck in

Loves: The warm, fuzzy feeling of seeing a clean beach

NEIL

HOW PLASTIC GETS IN THE OCEAN

10.

6.

5.

3.

9.

7.

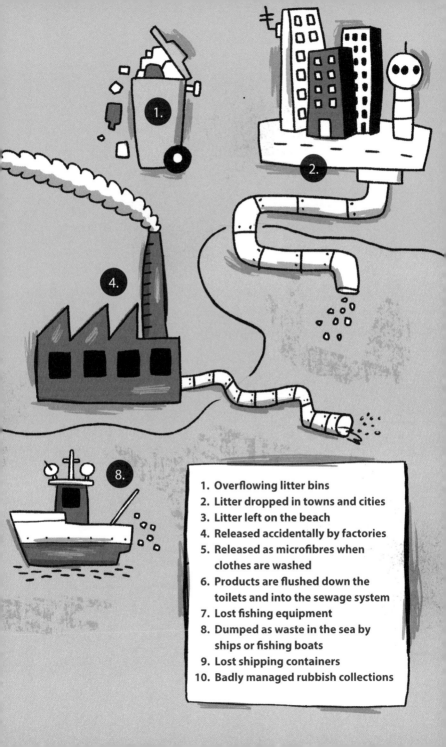

1. Overflowing litter bins
2. Litter dropped in towns and cities
3. Litter left on the beach
4. Released accidentally by factories
5. Released as microfibres when clothes are washed
6. Products are flushed down the toilets and into the sewage system
7. Lost fishing equipment
8. Dumped as waste in the sea by ships or fishing boats
9. Lost shipping containers
10. Badly managed rubbish collections

FIGHT PLASTIC IN YOUR SCHOOL BAG

What do superheroes keep in their school bags?
Can I guess? I bet you have a couple of pencils in there.
But how about felt-tip pens or ballpoints? What about old
crisp packets? School books? Textbooks? A ruler? Sweet
wrappers? An odd glove, perhaps. And definitely a reusable
water bottle. Am I right? This mission is going to help you
remove unnecessary plastic from your school bag.

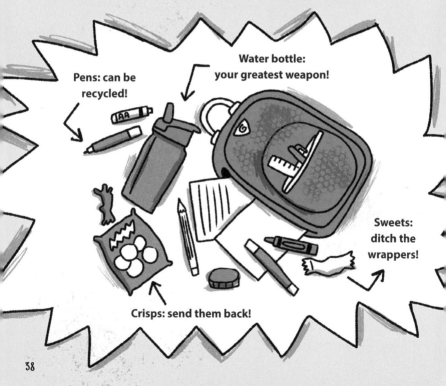

Pens: can be recycled!

Water bottle: your greatest weapon!

Sweets: ditch the wrappers!

Crisps: send them back!

BUST THE BALLPOINTS

Did you know that around 15 million ballpoint pens are sold around the world every day? Ballpoint pens are made of plastic and metal and are hard to recycle. Bic biros are designed to be disposable – when they run out, you throw them away. Over 200 million Bic ballpoint pens are sold each year in the UK. It's up to you to ensure they don't get to landfill.

A TRAIL OF WASTE:
Between 1950 and 2005, Bic, one of the world's biggest makers of pens, sold more than 100 billion plastic ballpoint pens. That's enough to draw a line to the moon and back more than 320,000 times.

Power to the pen!

YOUR 2 MINUTE MISSION:
Have a pen amnesty! Ask all your friends to empty their school bags and collect up their old pens. Then get a teacher to help you send them via www.terracycle.co.uk to Bic, who will recycle them. AND you can earn points (and money) for your school in the process.
80 POINTS

WHY YOUR WATER BOTTLE IS THE BEST THING EVER!

Your reusable water bottle is your best weapon in the fight against plastic. Every time you refill it, you are doing something great. So keep it up! Turn on the tap, reduce your plastic waste and help the ocean.

- On average, you go to school for 190 days a year for fourteen years. If you use a reusable water bottle every day, you are saving 2,660 bottles over the course of your school life.

- Tap water is 500 times cheaper than bottled water, and for you, at school, it's FREE.

EVERYDAY SUPERHERO

Name: Deb

Job: Teacher

Superpower: Turns little ideas into VERY big things

How you fight plastic: I invented ReFill water bottle stations

Top tip: Carry your water bottle with you wherever you go!

Hates: Single-use water bottles

Loves: Filling up my bottle for free at ReFill sites

DEB

- Tap water is healthier than fizzy drinks.

- You can drink as much tap water as you want. Keep filling that bottle!

- Plastic bottles and bottle tops make up 15% of beach litter.

- Most plastic bottles don't float (unless they have a top), so they sink to the bottom of the ocean, where they remain on the seabed.

- On the seabed, a drinks bottle can break down into thousands of pieces of microplastic.

- 35 million plastic bottles get used every day in the UK.

- Only about 57% of plastic bottles get recycled.

YOUR 2 MINUTE MISSION:
Does your school have a water fountain where you can fill your water bottle? Fill up! If not, how about starting a petition for a fountain at school? You could ask your parents and friends' parents to sign it too!
30 POINTS

DARN THOSE PESKY SWEET WRAPPERS

Back to your school bag. How many old sweet wrappers did you find in there?

The bad news: Did you know that a lot of sweet wrappers can't be recycled because of what they are made from? It's not great news, especially as superheroes need a little sugar rush every so often. (And, of course, only in moderation and under strictly controlled conditions.)

The good news: You don't have to have sweets in plastic wrappers! Some still come in paper and foil, including some chocolate and pastilles. Pick-and-mix sweets come in paper bags and travel sweets come in handy tins. The tins stop the sweets getting fluffy, are plastic-free and you can keep all your little stuff in them afterwards. Genius.

YOUR 2 MINUTE MISSION: **Sadly, if they come wrapped in plastic, it may be time to stop buying your old sweets. But it's also time to go sweet shopping. Get yourself some travel sweets in a tin! Raid the pick-and-mix! 10 POINTS**

CRISPS

Am I right in thinking you've had a packet of crisps recently?
What did you do with the packet afterwards? Bin it?
Sadly, until now that was the only thing we could do with them.

The bad news: Crisp packets are REALLY hard to recycle
because they are made from plastic and foil. Most of them go
to landfill. Shocked? Wait till you see the stats.

The worst news: Walkers, one of the world's biggest crisp
manufacturers, makes 11 million bags of crisps a day!
That's 4,004,000,000 bags of crisps a year (if they get a day off
at Christmas). In 2 minutes? 15,278 packets.

The good news: In 2018, Walkers teamed up with TerraCycle to
recycle and recover as many of their crisp packets as possible.
Now you can collect them, send them back and know they will
be turned into something else. And your school will benefit
because by collecting packets, you collect reward points too.

YOUR 2 MINUTE MISSION: **Collect all your crisp packets.
Collect all your friends' packets. With a teacher's
help, set up a crisp-packet recycling point. Send the
packets off to be recycled. Get points for your school.
Kaboom! No more waste! Find out more at
www.walkers.co.uk/recycle.
80 POINTS**

FIGHT PLASTIC IN YOUR LUNCH HOUR

When plastic affects us personally, it can be hard to make changes, especially if it means giving up tasty things you love. If your lunch is packed with good stuff, but packaged in plastic, you are going to have to make some difficult decisions. Are you ready to fight for your lunch? You are? Superhero status awaits!

EVERYDAY SUPERHERO

Name: Helford the Hero

Job: Common dolphin

Superpower: Super intelligence

How you fight plastic: I fought a plastic fishing line for hours before I was rescued

Top tip: Only eat fish that has been caught using dolphin-friendly nets

Hates: Humans leaving fishing nets in the sea

Loves: Playing with my pod

HELFORD THE HERO

TAKE A LOOK AT YOUR LUNCH

Superheroes eat lunch. That's a fact. But what's it packaged in?
Does your lunch come with a plastic fork? On a plastic plate?
With crisps? Do you have juice in a carton, with a straw? And
what about healthy bits? Do your carrots come ready-cut in a
plastic bag? It might be time for a change.

YOUR 2 MINUTE MISSION:
At your next lunch break,
ask three friends to show
you their lunches. Show
them yours. Do their
lunches contain
plastic? Make a
vow to cut out
AT LEAST one
piece of plastic
from lunch.
10 POINTS

So I hear
you've been
PACKING
PLASTIC,
Mr Lunchbox!

TAKE CONTROL OF YOUR PACKED LUNCH

Making packed lunches every day takes time and effort.
Often the easiest options are the worst for the planet.

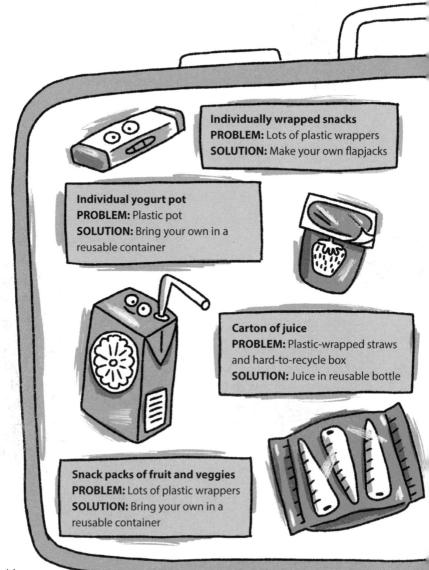

Individually wrapped snacks
PROBLEM: Lots of plastic wrappers
SOLUTION: Make your own flapjacks

Individual yogurt pot
PROBLEM: Plastic pot
SOLUTION: Bring your own in a
reusable container

Carton of juice
PROBLEM: Plastic-wrapped straws
and hard-to-recycle box
SOLUTION: Juice in reusable bottle

Snack packs of fruit and veggies
PROBLEM: Lots of plastic wrappers
SOLUTION: Bring your own in a
reusable container

Pre-cut apples, snack-sized chocolate bars, sandwiches, salads and juice cartons usually come packaged in lots of plastic.

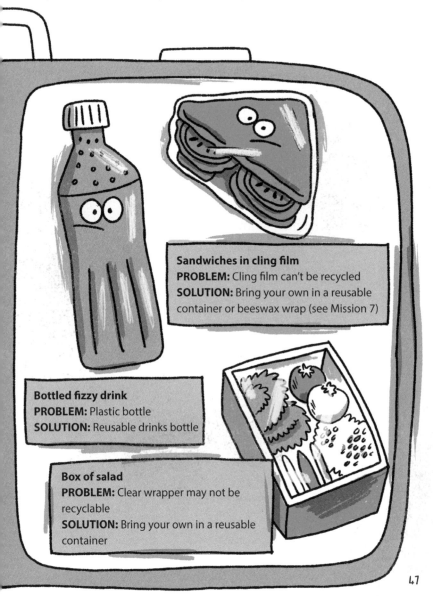

Sandwiches in cling film
PROBLEM: Cling film can't be recycled
SOLUTION: Bring your own in a reusable container or beeswax wrap (see Mission 7)

Bottled fizzy drink
PROBLEM: Plastic bottle
SOLUTION: Reusable drinks bottle

Box of salad
PROBLEM: Clear wrapper may not be recyclable
SOLUTION: Bring your own in a reusable container

FIGHT PLASTIC IN YOUR SCHOOL DINNER

How many school dinners get served in your school each day? If your school dinners get served with single-use plastic straws, plastic cutlery, cartons, plastic bottles or plastic containers, then it's not hard to do the maths and work out how much plastic your school could save by changing to non-plastic alternatives. It's time to fight for a plastic-free lunch!

Imagine how many lunches are served in your school over a school year.

Then imagine how many schools there are in the whole country.

YOUR 2 MINUTE MISSION: Show and tell! Ask your teacher if you can talk to your class or in assembly about your #2minutesuperhero mission. Explain why you are trying to reduce plastic and how you are doing it. Ask your fellow pupils to sign a pledge to help you.
50 POINTS

Think about how many
millions of school lunches
are eaten every year.

And remember, it
only takes one plastic
straw to kill a turtle.

YOUR 2 MINUTE MISSION: Does your school have a
recycling point for single-use plastics such as yogurt
pots, straws and drinks bottles? If not, set one up!
Get the permission of your teacher and headteacher.
Make labels so everyone can see what goes where.
40 POINTS

MISSION 6

FIGHT PLASTIC IN THE SUPERMARKET

This is where the fight against plastic gets serious. Why?
Because food and drink is one of the biggest sources of
single-use packaging. And the more we do to reduce our
reliance on it, the more we will fight plastic. But don't worry,
I will try to keep this part of your training fun. And short.

WHY DO SUPERMARKETS USE SO MUCH PLASTIC?
Supermarkets are full of plastic packaging for lots of reasons.

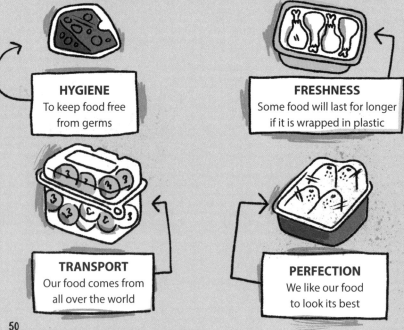

HYGIENE
To keep food free
from germs

FRESHNESS
Some food will last for longer
if it is wrapped in plastic

TRANSPORT
Our food comes from
all over the world

PERFECTION
We like our food
to look its best

HOW CAN YOU AVOID PLASTIC IN FOOD?

- Choose plastic-free fruit and veg
- Buy from local shops
- Buy from farmers' markets
- Take pots and tubs to the supermarket deli counter
- Always take your reusable bags!

CONVENIENCE
We like our food to be quick to prepare

PORTIONS
Single servings of food are easy to grab and go

MARKETING
Packaging can make us more likely to buy something

FIGHT PLASTIC WITH PESTER POWER

Do you get dragged around the supermarket? Good! Superheroes love it because it's a chance to get involved with the shopping. Pester your parents! Make a nuisance of yourself so your family makes the best possible choices when it comes to food. If there is an alternative that's not wrapped in plastic, get them to join you in your fight by changing what they buy!

YOUR 2 MINUTE MISSION:
Offer to help with the shopping and then you'll be able to have a say in the food you buy as a family.
20 POINTS

FIGHT PLASTIC BY MAKING SHOPPING DIFFERENT

Supermarkets are difficult places to fight plastic. So maybe it's time to go somewhere else! Farmers' markets are much more fun and are great places to buy fresh and local veg without all the wrapping.

You could also take your folks to a plastic-free shop or market, where you'll be able to pick up lots of dried goods, like flour, sugar, salt and cereals, without any kind of packaging. Don't forget your old takeaway containers!

YOUR 2 MINUTE MISSION: Go on a plastic-free shopping trip and come back with ZERO waste!
40 POINTS

FIGHT PLASTIC IN YOUR KITCHEN

Who runs the kitchen in your house? If you are really going to fight plastic in the kitchen you might need to stage a kitchen takeover. There are loads of things you can do to fight plastic in the kitchen. You can avoid food that comes in plastic, dabble in a bit of washing-up, start a VERY strict plastic-bag policy, learn to cook without plastic and help your family make better, plastic-free choices.

MAKE YOUR KITCHEN A BAG-FREE ZONE

How many bags are there under your kitchen sink? I bet there are loads!

It's your job to swap them for canvas bags you can use again and again. Don't let your family use anything else.

In 2015, a plastic-bag tax of 5p per bag was introduced in the UK. Before this tax was brought in, major UK retailers gave out the equivalent of 140 bags per person every year. After the tax was introduced it went down to just 25 per person per year. That's a drop of 82%.

This shows that small changes and actions can add up to make a BIG difference. Go, us!

YOUR 2 MINUTE MISSION:
You just got a new job.
You are the bag police!
Announce a zero tolerance
plastic-bag policy. Make
sure every member
of your family has NO
EXCUSE for using a plastic
bag. Put canvas bags in
the car, under the sink
and always to hand, then
charge each member of
your family 10p for every
plastic bag they use.
20 POINTS

EVERYDAY SUPERHERO

Name: Jim

Job: Lifeguard

Superpower: Drives a jet ski

How you fight plastic: I held a 14-hour beach clean-up from dawn until dusk

Top tip: Ditch plastic bags. They get caught in my jet ski engine, stopping me from rescuing people.

Hates: Plastic bags. You don't need them!

Loves: Telling people about the problems with single-use plastic

JIM

FREE THE WASHING-UP FROM PLASTIC

Washing-up intervention! Does your family use scourers or buy washing-up liquid? That's your chance to fight plastic! Most pot-scourers are made from plastic, so every time you wash up with them, tiny bits of plastic go down the sink and eventually into the sea. Every time you use a J-cloth or a man-made cloth you risk washing hundreds of tiny plastic fibres into the ocean.

YOUR 2 MINUTE MISSION: **Trade plastic scourers for coconut husk or metal ones, use cotton dishcloths instead of plastic ones and refill your washing-up liquid bottle at your local eco or plastic-free shop. 30 POINTS**

FIGHT PLASTIC WITH YOUR SUPERHERO SAUCEPAN

Can you cook? It might be time to learn. Cooking with fresh ingredients (that don't come in plastic packaging) is much better for the planet than eating food that comes in masses of packaging like ready meals, pots of soup or salads in plastic bags. Cook with loose vegetables and you'll reduce your plastic consumption straight away. Learning to bake cakes, bread and pizza bases will also help with your plastic consumption. And cooking can be a lot of fun too. Whoop!

GIVE UP THE MINI PORTIONS

Food that comes in individual portions – like small pots of yogurt and snack-sized food – uses more than double the amount of plastic. Say no! You can scoop yogurt out of a big pot, eat biscuits from a big pack and have cereal from a giant box. Easy!

YOUR 2 MINUTE MISSION: **Choose your favourite cereal. Find the biggest and smallest boxes of it that you can. Work out how many bowls of cereal each box contains and how many boxes of each size you'd need to fill 100 bowls.**
10 POINTS

FIGHT THE CLING FILM

Food wrap, such as cling film, is unrecyclable. So how about having a fun afternoon making an alternative that's 100% natural, reusable, easy to make and keeps food just as fresh for just as long?

YOUR 2 MINUTE MISSION: Make beeswax wraps with an adult. Find your brightest cotton fabric and paint it with beeswax (buy it online). If you are vegan, use plant-based wax. You can add pine resin to make the wraps sticky. 40 POINTS

HOW TO MAKE BEESWAX WRAPS

1. Get an adult to help. Cut 25cm x 25cm squares out of old, washed cotton fabric – maybe an old school shirt.
2. Melt beeswax pellets or beads (around 100g makes about 10 wraps) in a bowl sitting over another bowl of hot water. When the wax has melted, add a dessert spoon of coconut oil (this makes the wraps more flexible).
3. Put one square of fabric on a baking tray lined with parchment. With an old clean brush, paint the melted beeswax onto one side.
4. Carefully put the baking tray in a hot oven (around 140°C) for about a minute.
5. Using oven gloves, take the tray out of the oven. Remove the fabric by attaching 2 clothes pegs to the top corners.
6. Hold it over the tray for 2 minutes to let it cool.
7. Leave it to dry on a wire tray for 5 minutes.
8. After you've used the wrap, wash in cool water, then be awesome and reuse!

FIGHT PLASTIC IN YOUR GARDEN

Are you ready to get mucky? Superheroes with green fingers are going to love this mission. Why? Because it's all about fighting plastic in the garden and how you can use old plastic to grow new plants. And it's going to get messy. Brilliant!

MAKING COMPOST

Compost is the best kind of material for growing plants. Plants love it because it's made from rotted-down matter that is full of natural goodness.

It's easy to make compost at home, if you have space, although it does take time – more than 2 minutes!

If you can't make your own, you can often buy it from your local council. It will be made from food and garden waste that gets collected from your community. Sometimes it's free!

HOW TO MAKE COMPOST

1. Get a compost bin from your local council or make your own.

2. Collect your vegetable peelings, and green matter from your garden.

3. Put it in your compost bin.

4. Turn it over every couple of weeks to help it rot.

5. Ta-da! Compost!

SAVING PLASTIC BY GROWING

Growing plants is fun and often easier than you think. And growing your own can save you having to buy veg or salad from the supermarket. A lot of shop-bought salad comes in bags or wrappers that cannot be recycled, so it makes good sense to grow salad at home so you can cut down on plastic waste. Plus it's good for you. And tasty too.

HOW TO GROW SALAD AT HOME

1. Get some mixed salad seeds.

2. Fill a large, clean, black plastic food carton with compost.

3. Spread the seeds across the top. Cover with another thin layer of compost.

4. Place on a sunny window sill. Water gently. Wait for about 10 days. Keep watered.

5. Cut the salad leaves when they are small. Leave them to grow some more. Cut again.

REUSING PLASTIC

Sadly there is still a lot of single-use plastic out there. Gardening is a great way of reusing it. Yogurt pots, plastic food containers and plastic bottles are all brilliant for growing seeds.

YOUR 2 MINUTE MISSION: Cut a clear plastic bottle in half and fill the bottom with compost. Push three pea seeds around the bottle's edge. Water and leave on a window sill. You'll be able to see the seeds germinate and the seedlings grow. When they're big enough, plant them outside in a larger pot. Either cut and add the pea shoots to your salad or wait to eat the peas. 20 POINTS

EVERYDAY SUPERHERO

Name: Dr Seaweed

Job: Gardener

Superpower: Green fingers

How you fight plastic: I reuse plastic pots and containers in my garden

Top tip: Start a compost heap so you can grow plants from your old veg peelings

Hates: Waste that doesn't get used up

Loves: Seeing new life grow

DR SEAWEED

START A GARDENING CLUB

If you can't start a garden at home, get help starting a gardening club at school or in your community. Start small by planting simple veg, such as tomatoes, and then move on from there. Before long you could have a jungle, market garden or farm!

YOUR 2 MINUTE MISSION: **Talk to your teacher about starting a gardening club or growing salad or veg in your classroom. Bring in leftover plastic pots, trays and containers and then take the veg home when it's big enough to eat.**
20 POINTS

FIGHT PLASTIC IN YOUR BATHROOM

The bathroom is a great place to fight plastic. Why? Because there is so much of it in there! Many bathroom products, from soap to shampoo, are either made from or come packaged in plastic. It might seem like a difficult task to switch to something that isn't plastic, but it can be done! In fact, these 2 minute missions are easier than you might think.

BATHROOM PLASTICS LAID BARE

- Around 33 million people in the UK use a standard toothbrush made from plastic.

- Every year in the UK we dispose of around 130 million toothbrushes!

- The UK gets through 13.2 billion cotton buds and 10.8 billion wet wipes a year.

- Cotton-bud sticks are one of the top items found on beach cleans. They are small enough to escape the sewage system and get washed out to sea.

Toothbrushes are almost always plastic. But they don't have to be.

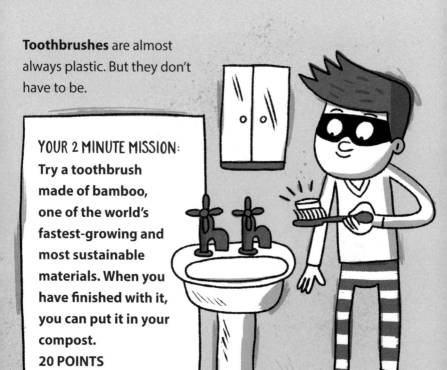

YOUR 2 MINUTE MISSION:
Try a toothbrush made of bamboo, one of the world's fastest-growing and most sustainable materials. When you have finished with it, you can put it in your compost.
20 POINTS

Toothpaste usually comes in plastic tubes. Again, it doesn't have to. Some brands come in metal tubes that can easily be recycled and some come in tablet form or in glass jars.

YOUR 2 MINUTE MISSION: **Try toothpaste that comes in a glass jar or in tablet form. It might not be what you are used to but it will work and is a fab way to fight plastic twice a day!**
20 POINTS

Squirty soap comes in plastic bottles – some can be refilled, others just get thrown away or recycled when they are empty. Also, the plastic pumps can be hard to recycle as they have springs inside.

YOUR 2 MINUTE MISSION: **Change your soap! Get rid of the squirty stuff and replace it with a bar of solid soap that comes wrapped in paper.**
10 POINTS

Shampoo, conditioner and shower gel come in single-use plastic bottles. While they can be recycled, it's better to do without.

YOUR 2 MINUTE MISSION: **Try out a solid shampoo bar and use solid soap instead of shower gel.**
10 POINTS

Toilet roll isn't made of plastic, but often comes wrapped in plastic.

> **YOUR 2 MINUTE MISSION: At your local supermarket, try to find toilet paper that comes wrapped in paper.**
> **10 POINTS**

Cotton buds often have plastic sticks.

> **YOUR 2 MINUTE MISSION: Look for cotton buds with paper sticks. Buy these instead.**
> **10 POINTS**

★ EVERYDAY SUPERHERO

Name: Rowena

Job: Make-up designer

Superpower: Makes waste-free smellies

How you fight plastic: I create soaps and shampoos that don't come in bottles

Top tip: Shampoo bars last ages and produce no plastic litter

Hates: Things not getting reused

Loves: Living on a clean, tidy planet

ROWENA

FIGHT PLASTIC IN YOUR LOO

Who's up for a visit to the sewage works? Bring a clothes peg. It might get stinky. This is where all your wee and poo goes after you flush the loo. Sadly, it's where lots of other stuff ends up too. And that's a problem for the ocean.

THINK BEFORE YOU FLUSH

Whenever you flush your loo, everything in the toilet bowl goes down your U-bend, into the sewers and down to the sewage treatment plant, where it gets filtered and cleaned.

The trouble is that the filters at the sewage plants can't catch everything. Small things, like cotton-bud sticks, escape and make their way through the water system and out to sea. Wet wipes – which are made of plastic – get caught up in the sewage system or in fatbergs, which are giant lumps of congealed fat that form from grease and oil that have been poured down people's sinks.

WHEN THINGS GET SMELLY

When extremely heavy rain means there is too much water for the sewage system to process, water companies relieve the pressure by releasing raw sewage through huge pipes called combined sewer overflows (CSOs). All the pee, poo, puke and paper and anything else that's been flushed goes straight out to sea and can eventually end up on the beach. That means all the plasters, cotton buds, wet wipes and tampon applicators end up on MY BEACH. We pick them up all the time and it is horrible!

YOUR 2 MINUTE MISSION: **Ask your teacher to organize a visit to your local sewage treatment plant. It might not sound like fun but it'll be VERY interesting. 100 POINTS**

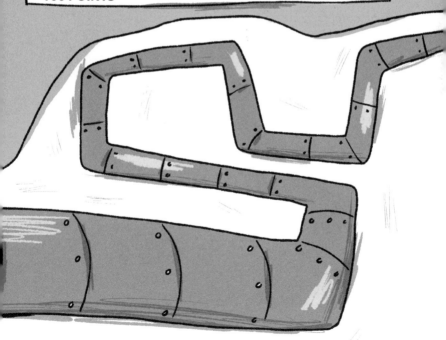

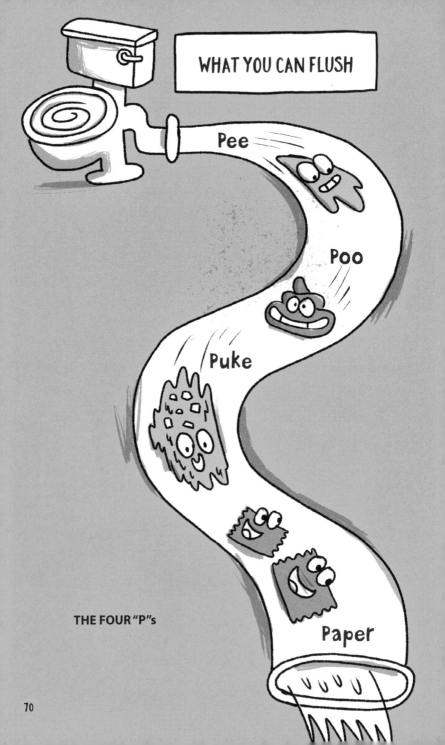

WHAT YOU CAN FLUSH

Pee

Poo

Puke

Paper

THE FOUR "P"s

WHAT YOU CAN'T FLUSH

Cotton-bud sticks

Wet wipes

Glitter

Microbeads

Toy soldiers

Plastic bags

Women's hygiene products

Plasters

Pads

Bandages

ANYTHING THAT'S NOT ONE OF THE FOUR "P"s

LOVE YOUR LOO

Remember that only pee, paper, puke and poo can go down the loo!

YOUR 2 MINUTE MISSION: **Count up the number of loos that you use regularly. Make a sign for each one that says: ONLY PEE, PAPER, PUKE AND POO DOWN THIS LOO – THANK YOU!**
20 POINTS

Find out from your family what they flush down the loo.

YOUR 2 MINUTE MISSION: **If your family flushes anything down the loo that isn't one of the FOUR "P"s, ask if you can put a bin – with a lid – next to the loo, for everything else. These items can then go in the rubbish or be recycled.**
20 POINTS

FACTBERG: In 2018, a 64-metre-long fatberg – a lump of wet wipes, grease and oils from kitchen waste – was found in the sewers of Sidmouth, Devon. That's longer than six double-decker buses!

Wet wipes are often made from plastic and should never be flushed. We find lots of them on beach cleans. The thing is, a flannel will do the job just as well, and it can be reused!

YOUR 2 MINUTE MISSION: **If your family uses wet wipes, make a notice for your loo reminding everyone not to flush them!**
10 POINTS

EVERYDAY SUPERHERO

Name: Shayna

Job: Flesh-footed shearwater

Superpower: Dodging fishermen

How you fight plastic: I went on telly with a stomach full of plastic

Top tip: DON'T FLUSH IT! Plastic looks and tastes like food to seabirds.

Hates: Being made to be sick to get rid of plastic

Loves: Being rescued and not having a stomach full of plastic

SHAYNA

FIGHT PLASTIC IN YOUR WARDROBE

I know what you are thinking! You're thinking that there's no plastic in your wardrobe, aren't you? Believe it or not, your wardrobe – or floordrobe, if that's where you keep your clothes – is a good place to fight plastic. Lots of clothes are made from man-made fibres which are plastic, including nylon, Lycra and polyester. And when they are washed, plastic clothes shed lots of tiny fibres, called microfibres, that go down drains to the sea.

WHY PLASTIC IS THE NEW OLD

Nylon, polyester, acrylic and other synthetic fibres (that don't come from nature) are all made from different types of polymers (plastics) and won't break down or biodegrade. Football shirts, school blazers, sports socks and outdoor jackets are often made from man-made fibres. You can easily check what materials have been used by looking at the labels.

It's the same with sparkly stuff like sequins. Sadly they are made from plastic and are very difficult to recycle. Fake fur trims on coats are also made from synthetic fibres.

You can avoid plastic in your clothes by choosing natural alternatives, like wool, cotton, hemp, silk or bamboo.

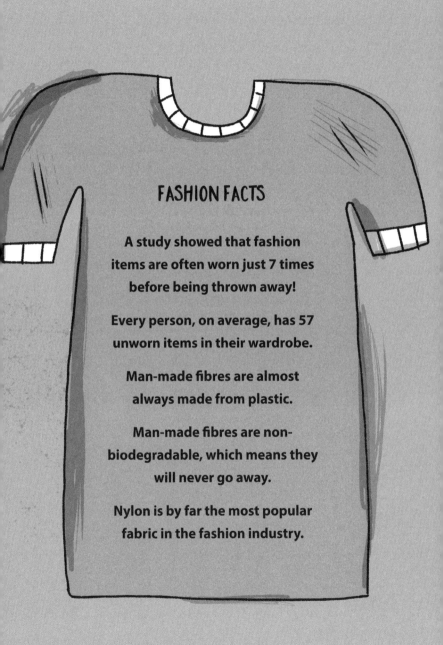

FASHION FACTS

A study showed that fashion items are often worn just 7 times before being thrown away!

Every person, on average, has 57 unworn items in their wardrobe.

Man-made fibres are almost always made from plastic.

Man-made fibres are non-biodegradable, which means they will never go away.

Nylon is by far the most popular fabric in the fashion industry.

WHY WASHING CLOTHES IS BAD FOR YOU

Microfibres are tiny plastic fibres that come off your clothes when you wash them. They are one of the biggest sources of plastics in the ocean. Imagine the fluff in your tumble dryer going down the drain each time you wash your clothes! Eeek. Sewage treatment plants are unable to catch the fibres so they go straight into a river or the sea. The fibres don't break down and instead are eaten by plankton and tiny fish. If those fish are eaten by bigger fish, the fibres move up the food chain, and can potentially be eaten by us. Yuck!

THE GOOD: NATURAL FIBRES

Blue jeans made of cotton

Jumpers made of wool

Hawaiian shirts made of viscose

Undies made of bamboo

EVERYDAY SUPERHERO

Name: Linda

Job: Fashion designer

Superpower: Turns rubbish into beautiful clothes

How you fight plastic: I reuse ocean plastic by making dresses

Top tip: Don't look the other way!

Hates: Companies pretending to be green to sell more products

Loves: Fighting plastic together

LINDA

THE BAD: MAN-MADE FIBRES

Football shirts made of nylon (sorry)

Jumpers made of acrylic

Fleeces made of polyester

Socks made of nylon

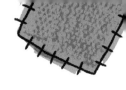

HOW TO FIGHT PLASTIC IN YOUR WARDROBE

The secret to fighting plastic in your wardrobe is to choose your clothes carefully and make them last by loving them for as long as you can before buying new ones. Here are some other ideas:

1. Learn how to sew! Sewing up holes will stop your clothes from wearing out, which means you'll be able to wear them again and again and again.

> **YOUR 2 MINUTE MISSION: Learn how to sew up holes in your old clothes.**
> **10 POINTS**

2. Wash your nylon, polyester or man-made clothes less often. Less often means less plastic goes in the sea.

> **YOUR 2 MINUTE MISSION: Separate your clothes that are made from man-made fibres from those made of natural fibres. Wash them less often.**
> **10 POINTS**

3. Wash your man-made clothes in a special bag or with a ball that will catch the microfibres before they enter the water system.

YOUR 2 MINUTE MISSION: **Catch microfibres in the washing machine with a specially designed bag or ball. Bin the fibres.**
10 POINTS

4. Pass your old clothes on to a friend or relative, or send your old clothes to a charity shop or jumble sale. Just don't bin them!

YOUR 2 MINUTE MISSION: **Organize a clothes swap at school or at a club. Bring in the clothes you don't love any more and swap them for your friends' unloved clothes.**
10 POINTS

5. Get creative and try upcycling! Jazz up your old clothes with plastic-free dyes, fabric paint and extra bits.

YOUR 2 MINUTE MISSION: **Make yourself your very own #2minutesuperhero costume out of your old clothes.**
20 POINTS

FIGHT PLASTIC ON THE PITCH, COURT, TRACK AND COURSE

Sport is great! But plastic on the pitch is awful! As soon as it rains, any post-match litter could get washed down a drain, into a river and then out to sea. It's going to take a superhero to tackle the problem.

PLASTIC-FREE GAMES

Sporting legends need hydration and sustenance. And that means you! You need water and snacks on the pitch, whether you are playing hockey, running cross-country, cycling, swimming or kicking a ball about in the park. But remember to make sure your snacks and water are plastic-free!

RUNNING SCARES: At the London Marathon around 750,000 single-use plastic bottles are used.

YOUR 2 MINUTE MISSION:
Declare your sports events plastic-free. If you take snacks, go for homemade flapjacks or cakes, and ALWAYS remember to carry your reusable water bottle! 20 POINTS

CLEAR UP BEFORE AND AFTER KICK-OFF

Doing a **#2minutelitterpick** before you start your game will ensure your pitch is clean and safe. Then do it again afterwards, and leave your pitch or track nicer than it was when you arrived. If you do this when you go to play at other clubs or schools, they will be VERY impressed. You'll be showing them what to do!

YOUR 2 MINUTE MISSION: **Get your team to do a litter pick after every game. Take a bag and pick up any litter. Recycle what you can. You will look great and will be WINNING, whatever happens in the game. 30 POINTS**

EVERYDAY SUPERHERO

Name: Pete

Job: Cleans beaches

Superpower: Never giving up. Not ever. Not even when it seems impossible.

How you fight plastic: I lead a group of happy beach and street cleaners

Top tip: Being outside makes you happier. Walking on a clean beach is a very happy thing.

Hates: Horrid juice from old dustbins

Loves: Gadgets to put on my gadget belt

PETE

GO PLOGGING!

Plogging is a Scandinavian idea where joggers pick up litter as they run. It's very simple – you just run and pick up litter! Do it during the warm-up!

YOUR 2 MINUTE MISSION:
Grab a bag at lunchtime and go plogging around the playground!
30 POINTS

MISSION 13

FIGHT PLASTIC ON YOUR DAYS OUT

Now that you've got the superhero bug, your weekends and days out are going to be completely different! You'll see the world through new eyes, spotting litter, avoiding single-use plastic and making sure you leave places you go nicer than they were when you got there. What a fantastic thing! You are a #2minutesuperhero, making the world better wherever you go!

PLASTIC-FREE DAYS OUT

Going to the beach? Yay! Join me in a **#2minutebeachclean**. It's easy. Set a timer, grab a bag AND GO! How much plastic can you find? And if you're having an ice cream afterwards, treat yourself to a cone – for plastic-free licking!

YOUR 2 MINUTE MISSION: **Do a #2minutebeachclean and see what you find. Look for plastic bags, bottles, bottle tops, cotton-bud sticks, wet wipes and bits of fishing net. They are the most common items we find. But also look for Lego, toy soldiers, fishing lines and old flip-flops.**
10 POINTS

FIGHT PLASTIC AT THE CINEMA

Off to the movies? Take a paper straw and perhaps even your own reusable cup! Popcorn, of course, comes in cardboard boxes, so you're good to go. Just watch out for the bags of sweets and plastic cutlery. Take your litter home instead of leaving it – then you can recycle it!

> **YOUR 2 MINUTE MISSION:**
> **Make it a plastic-free film night!**
> **10 POINTS**

FIGHT PLASTIC AT THE THEME PARK

Going to a theme park? It can be a challenge! But you can do it. Take sandwiches, your reusable water bottle and your own homemade snacks to enjoy a plastic-free rollercoaster of a day out. Say no to plastic straws or take your own paper one.

MAKING FAST FOOD PLASTIC-FREE

Fast food doesn't have to be plastic food. Refuse plastic straws and cutlery if you are offered them, choose cups without lids and say no to those horrible plastic sauce sachets and pots.

FAST FUTURES? The EU is clamping down on single-use plastics from fast-food chains. So expect a plastic-free – and happier – meal soon!

SLEEP WELL ON YOUR SLEEPOVERS

Going to stay at other people's houses for parties and sleepovers doesn't mean you can't be plastic-free. Remember your reusable water bottle and pack a plastic tub for your slice of the cake. Sweet dreams!

EVERYDAY SUPERHERO

Name: The Super Whale

Job: Humpback whale

Superpower: Sings songs that can be heard for hundreds of miles

How you fight plastic: I battled a plastic fishing net twice – and won! – with help from British Divers Marine Life Rescue

Top tip: Don't swim near nets

Hates: Being tangled up in rope

Loves: Swimming in a clean ocean

THE SUPER WHALE

FIGHT PLASTIC WITH YOUR POCKET MONEY

If you're anything like the average superhero, you get a whopping £262.60 in pocket money each year. That's an average of £5.05 a week. You get it on Saturdays. And you save about 70% of it. Am I right?

That means you spend some of it. And that's important. How you spend your money is vital in the fight against plastic. You can vote for a better world by making clever buying choices.

SUPERHERO SPENDING

If you play your cards right, you could even get money for being a superhero! How? You might earn money for doing chores, such as cleaning the kitchen and bathroom, helping with the shopping or even doing the gardening. As part of your superhero training, you'll be doing all those things anyway! So why not use your superhero training to boost your pocket money?

SWEETS

BOOKS

TOYS

TECHNOLOGY

SAVINGS

GAMES

COMICS AND
MAGAZINES

SHOW THE WORLD BY BUYING WELL

What do you normally spend your money on? Your pocket money is your chance to show everyone – with your own money – what you want the world to be like. You can send a strong message to companies by choosing not to buy toys or sweets that are wrapped in plastic, or made from plastic (the toys, not the sweets!). Also don't buy comics and magazines that are wrapped in plastic or come with plastic toys. You don't want things that are likely to break or be quickly discarded.

YOUR 2 MINUTE MISSION: **Stop spending your pocket money on one item that contains plastic. If it's sweets, go to a pick-and-mix instead. If it's toys, buy something that is plastic-free and you will keep. 20 POINTS**

BUYING PLASTIC-FREE SWEETS

You don't have to buy sweets wrapped in plastic. Take a trip to a pick-and-mix where they sell sweets individually. Just beware of plastic packaging. You could even take your own bags or containers! Sweets come in travel tins too.

Oh, and avoid those egg-shaped sweets that have plastic toys inside. You know the ones I mean! They are AWFUL for the planet.

BUYING TOYS FOR LIFE

Lots of toys are made of plastic. The secret here is to buy toys that you will use for a long time – and can then sell or give away later. So that means buying carefully, saving for something more expensive, finding things that won't break easily and that you know you'll play with loads.

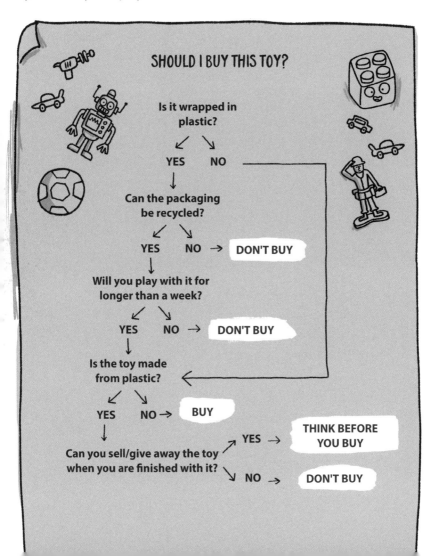

SHOULD I BUY THIS TOY?

Is it wrapped in plastic?

YES   NO

Can the packaging be recycled?

YES   NO → DON'T BUY

Will you play with it for longer than a week?

YES   NO → DON'T BUY

Is the toy made from plastic?

YES   NO → BUY

Can you sell/give away the toy when you are finished with it?

YES → THINK BEFORE YOU BUY

NO → DON'T BUY

EARN MONEY FROM YOUR OLD STUFF

You can boost your pocket money by selling toys, clothes, games and books that you no longer need or want. This also means that you can make sure your stuff goes to a good home and will be reused. Throwing things away just because you have finished with them is crazy – especially when someone else might love them.

Sites like eBay, Gumtree and Preloved are great for selling old toys, books and games, while ASOS Marketplace and Vinted are places you can sell old clothes. Get your family to help you.

WHAT TO DO WITH YOUR OLD STUFF

CLOTHES

Sell on auction sites

Donate to shops and get a discount

Give to charity

BOOKS

Sell online

Sell at school bring-and-buy sales

Donate to charity

TOYS

Sell online

Give to relatives

Donate to children's charities or toy libraries

YOUR 2 MINUTE MISSION: Ask your school to organize a bring-and-buy sale, where you and your friends can sell your unwanted books, toys and clothes – and earn money too!
40 POINTS

FIGHT PLASTIC BY MENDING IT

If one of your toys breaks, mend it! It's pretty simple. Don't just throw it away. Nowadays there are places called repair cafés where you can get your old stuff mended so you can keep on using it. This is great because it means you don't have to buy something new and you can keep loving your old stuff for longer.

FIGHT PLASTIC IN YOUR CELEBRATIONS

How many sleeps until Christmas? Easter? Halloween?
I can't wait! But sadly, these celebration days have become
an all-out plastic fest of wastefulness. If you want to fight
plastic, you're going to have to do Christmas, Halloween
and Easter a bit differently. The good news though?
You don't have to give up the Easter eggs.

WE WILL NOT CANCEL CHRISTMAS

Great news! Christmas is all about giving and being together.
But somewhere along the way it's become about stuff and
tinsel and plastic wrapping. It's time to reclaim Christmas.

WASTEFUL FACT: It is estimated that around 125,000
tonnes of plastic waste is created in the UK each Christmas.

FIGHT PLASTIC WITH YOUR PRESENTS

The giving of gifts is a symbolic gesture. So save your pocket money and make a homemade gift instead of buying something made of plastic or packaged in plastic. Make fudge or bake biscuits. Give a gift with love – the ocean will thank you.

YOUR 2 MINUTE MISSION: **Make presents for your family and wrap them in paper, newspaper or paper you have decorated yourself. Tie them up with string (sticky tape is plastic!).**
30 POINTS

NO MORE PLASTIC WRAPPING

Lots of foil-backed and shiny wrapping paper is plastic. You can tell by scrunching it up. If it stays scrunched, it's paper. If it expands again, it's plastic. Go for the paper wrapping and you'll be able to recycle or reuse it later.

WRAP UP THE WASTE: An estimated 227,000 miles of wrapping paper gets sent to landfill each year.

A CHRISTMAS TREE FOR EVER

Each year we cut down millions of trees or buy fake ones made of plastic! What a waste. If you want an artificial tree, buy it second hand and reuse it every year. But if you can, buy a locally grown Christmas tree in a pot that you can bring inside and decorate each year. Better still, make your own tree out of driftwood or sticks.

DECORATING THE TREE

Great news! There are amazing plastic-free alternatives to tinsel, baubles and glittery decorations. You can decorate a tree brilliantly with biscuits, dried slices of lemon or orange, and paper chains. Homemade decorations are fun and easy to make too.

**YOUR 2 MINUTE MISSION: Make a paper chain to decorate your house. How long can you make it?
10 POINTS**

THE FIGHT-PLASTIC CHRISTMAS

Say no to:

- 🌲 Tinsel
- 🌲 Plastic baubles
- 🌲 Glittery decorations
- 🌲 Plastic and foil wrapping paper
- 🌲 Sticky tape
- 🌲 Gift bags
- 🌲 Shop-bought cards (especially ones with glitter)
- 🌲 Shop-bought crackers
- 🌲 Plastic packaging
- 🌲 Plastic straws
- 🌲 Single-use cups, plates and cutlery

LOVE A PLASTIC-FREE CHRISTMAS

Feel the festive joy with:

- 🌲 Real trees with roots
- 🌲 Paper chains made from old magazines and newspapers
- 🌲 Homemade decorations
- 🌲 Homemade crackers (with bad Dad jokes)
- 🌲 Homemade cards
- 🌲 Gummed tape and string
- 🌲 Wrapping paper made from newsprint or brown paper
- 🌲 Homebaked goods for pressies

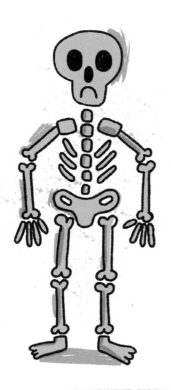

THE SCARY THING ABOUT HALLOWEEN?

It's not the ghouls. It's the plastic! Waste companies hate Halloween. There's just so much waste from discarded costumes, plastic skulls and scary decorative tat. So how about making a costume out of old clothes this year? I bet there are some horrors in your mum's wardrobe that you could use! For trick-or-treating, fill a bowl with chocolates and sweets wrapped in paper and foil instead of plastic wrappers. EASY!

THE FRIGHTENING TRUTH: It is estimated that around 12,500 tonnes of Halloween costumes are thrown out each year in the UK.

YOUR 2 MINUTE MISSION: **Make a Halloween costume out of things you wear every day. Or borrow something silly. A scary hairstyle or face paints can transform an outfit into something really terrifying. Make it your mission to have a plastic-free Halloween. 20 POINTS**

A PLASTIC-FREE EASTER

I'm still confused about Easter. What is the Easter bunny for? And why do we give eggs? Oh yes! It's to celebrate spring and new life. Given that plastic is hurting our wildlife, we need to think about plastic at Easter really carefully.

Let me out!

OUT WITH THE PLASTIC!

Lots of Easter eggs are over-packaged, with plastic inserts holding eggs in place. But some aren't! You can still buy eggs in cardboard and tin foil. Both are 100% recyclable.

EGGSTRA WASTE: Around 148 million Easter eggs are sold each year in the UK, producing over 3,000 tonnes of plastic waste.

YOUR 2 MINUTE MISSION: Make sure the chocolate you eat this Easter is not covered in plastic. Choose your eggs wisely!
10 POINTS

THE FIGHT-PLASTIC PARTY!

It's time to celebrate. You're nearly at the end of your plastic-fighting odyssey and your superhero status awaits. So it's time to PARTY! I like plastic-free parties where there is no waste. Other than things to recycle, there's nothing left afterwards except brilliant memories, sleepy eyes and exhausted dancing feet. Are you ready? It's the Fight-Plastic Party for all the #2minutesuperheroes!

YOUR 2 MINUTE MISSION: Next time you have a birthday party or celebration, make it a FIGHT-PLASTIC PARTY! Plan carefully. Make your own decorations and cook up a party-food fiesta! Use the lists in this mission to help you.
150 POINTS

THE EVIL PARTY VILLAINS

- **Party poppers:** sorry, team, I am a party popper party pooper. They are plastic! Yuck.

- **Balloons:** sadly you're going to have to pop your balloon habit. Balloons, even those that claim to be biodegradable, are a menace to wildlife.

- **Glitter:** glitter is fun… But the minute it goes down the drain, it becomes a dangerous microplastic that washes straight into the sea.

- **Party bags:** you must resist the plastic party bag. Avoid plastic toys, cling film around the cake and individually wrapped sweets and snacks such as lollipops.

- **Party food:** so much party food comes in plastic packaging. From sausage rolls to traybakes, supermarkets seem to manage to give you more plastic than party. Fight back!

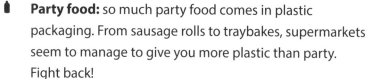

- **Plastic plates and cutlery:** no, no, no, no, no! Plastic plates, knives, forks and spoons may be recyclable but it is better to do without.

- **Straws:** party people always say no to plastic straws.

BUBBLE-BURSTING FACT: To turtles, balloons and plastic bags look just like jellyfish – their favourite food.

EVERYDAY SUPERHERO

Name: Bob

Job: Green turtle

Superpower: Swims over 1,500 miles to nest and breed

How you fight plastic: I was rescued and then made to poo out all the balloons and plastic bags I'd eaten

Top tip: Don't let go of balloons! Even the biodegradable ones can be harmful.

Hates: That balloons look like food

Loves: Delicious seagrasses

BOB

THE GOOD GUYS

- **Homemade decorations:** paper chains and lanterns are easy and fun to make. And the best thing? You can recycle them!

- **Bunting:** paper bunting made from string and coloured paper or magazines is cool. You can also sew some from old material and ribbon!

- **Paper table decorations:** newsprint paper – which you can buy in rolls at hobby shops – is fab for using as tablecloths and wrapping paper. Put crayons on the tables and invite your friends to graffiti!

- **Paper party bags:** this is easy to sort out right here and now! Use brown paper bags, kitchen roll to wrap your cake, and plastic-free toys such as notebooks, masks and pencils.

- **Real party food:** it's easy to avoid plastic-wrapped party food. But you might have to work at it. Make your own sandwiches, muffins, flapjacks and cakes!

- **Plates and cutlery:** you don't need plastic plates when you could use real plates and wash them up afterwards... Imagine! If you need more, borrow them from friends.

- **Straws:** do not party without straws. You don't have to! You can buy paper straws from the supermarket, which is fantastic!

EVERYDAY SUPERHERO

Name: Dolly

Job: Online campaigner

Superpower: Technology

How you fight plastic: I run online campaigns to stop people releasing balloons and buying plastic

Top tip: Buy less, use less and reuse stuff more

Hates: Balloons and sports cap bottle tops

Loves: Picnics on the beach

DOLLY

FIGHT PLASTIC WITH YOUR VOICE

Well done for completing the #2minutesuperhero training! But there is one final mission before you're done. It's very simple and can make a massive difference because it will let the people in power know what you think about plastic.

YOUR 2 MINUTE MISSION: Write a letter or an email to someone who is responsible for making decisions that affect your fight against plastic. It could be a Member of Parliament, a local councillor, a teacher or your headteacher. Tell them what worries you about plastic, what you need them to do and why. Use the template opposite to get started.
Go for it! Your voice matters.
100 POINTS

Find your local councillor here:
www.mysociety.org/wehelpyou/contact-your-local-councillor
Find your local MP here: **www.theyworkforyou.com**

Dear [Name]

My name is [add your name] and I am [your age] years old. I attend [name your school here] and I am writing to you about plastic.

I am very worried about the health of our oceans and I am also worried about my future, due to the overuse, production and bad management of plastic. I believe that we have to do all we can to stop plastic entering the oceans by recycling more, stopping plastic at the source and using less of it in our daily lives.

I have taken a pledge to fight plastic and I now want you to do your bit to help. I want you to fine companies that pollute the oceans. I need you to bring in laws to stop companies giving the public unnecessary plastic and encourage companies to use recycled plastic in all their products.

We also need an immediate ban on ALL single-use plastics and a simple recycling system that is the same for everyone, wherever you live. We need it now.

Can you do this for me and my future?
I hope so. Please reply with your pledge for plastic.

Yours
[sign your name here]

MISSION COMPLETED

Close your eyes...

Imagine standing on a spotless beach, staring out at a vast ocean, free of plastic, pulsing with life, surf and wonder. Whales are blowing waterspouts, dolphins are spinning. Flying fish skim across the sunlit surface of the water. Beneath the waves, fish and seals are dancing. Above you, seabirds squawk and squabble. Pufflings fly, for the first time, flapping madly against the breeze, as pufflings do.

You can smell the fresh air and the seaweed, feel a warm wind on your skin, taste the salt on your lips and hear the crashing of the waves.

The ocean is beautiful and you are a part of it, wherever you live. A turtle pops up, just in front of you, surprising you a little. It smiles and says, "Thank you!"

You did that.
How does it feel?
YOU ARE A #2MINUTESUPERHERO.
MISSION COMPLETED.

YOUR
SUPERHERO
RATING...

SUPERHERO POINTS

Now that you've finished your training, it's time to find out what kind of superhero you are. Add up the points you've earned by completing your missions.

MISSION 1: GET TO KNOW THE BAD STUFF

Find five pieces of good plastic that you use every day.

10 POINTS

Find five pieces of bad plastic that will only be used once before being thrown away.

20 POINTS

TOTAL MISSION POINTS: 30

MISSION 2: FIGHT PLASTIC IN YOUR BIN

Get a food waste bin and start a compost heap. Find out how to make compost in Mission 8.

30 POINTS

Make a bin chart and mark it each time anyone takes out a bin bag. Monitor how many rubbish bags your family puts out each week and see if you can cut it in half.

50 POINTS

Visit a Materials Recovery Facility (MRF) near you.

50 POINTS

Find three straws – one that is plastic, one that is biodegradable plastic and one that is paper. Get a plant pot and fill it with mud. Then poke the straws halfway into the mud. Leave them for a couple of weeks and see what happens!

20 POINTS

TOTAL MISSION POINTS: 150

MISSION 3: FIGHT PLASTIC IN YOUR PARK

Do a **#2minutelitterpick**. On your walk home from school or at the park, spend 2 minutes filling an old carrier bag with litter. Recycle what you can and bin the rest. How much did you get in 2 minutes?

20 POINTS

TOTAL MISSION POINTS: 20

MISSION 4: FIGHT PLASTIC IN YOUR SCHOOL BAG

Have a pen amnesty! Ask all your friends to empty their school bags and collect up their old pens. Then get a teacher to help you send them via **www.terracycle.co.uk** to Bic, who will recycle them. AND you can earn points (and money) for your school in the process.

80 POINTS

Does your school have a water fountain where you can fill your water bottle? Fill up! If not, how about starting a petition for a fountain at school? You could ask your parents and your friends' parents to sign it too!

30 POINTS

Sadly, if they come wrapped in plastic, it may be time to stop buying your old sweets. But it's also time to go sweet shopping. Get yourself travel sweets in a tin! Raid the pick-and-mix!

10 POINTS

Collect all your crisp packets. Collect all your friends' packets. With a teacher's help, set up a crisp-packet recycling point. Send the packets off to be recycled. Get points for your school. Kaboom! No more waste! Find out more at **www.walkers.co.uk/recycle**.

80 POINTS

TOTAL MISSION POINTS: 200

MISSION 5: FIGHT PLASTIC IN YOUR LUNCH HOUR

At your next lunch break, ask three friends to show you their lunches. Show them yours. Do their lunches contain plastic? Make a vow to cut out AT LEAST one piece of plastic from lunch.

10 POINTS

Show and tell! Ask your teacher if you can talk to your class or in assembly about your **#2minutesuperhero** mission. Explain why you are trying to reduce plastic and how you are doing it. Ask your fellow pupils to sign a pledge to help you.

50 POINTS

Does your school have a recycling point for single-use plastics such as yogurt pots, straws and drinks bottles? If not, set one up! Get the

permission of your teacher and headteacher. Make labels so everyone can see what goes where.

40 POINTS

TOTAL MISSION POINTS: 100

MISSION 6: FIGHT PLASTIC IN THE SUPERMARKET

Offer to help with the shopping and then you'll be able to have a say in the food you buy as a family.

20 POINTS

Go on a plastic-free shopping trip and come back with ZERO waste!

40 POINTS

TOTAL MISSION POINTS: 60

MISSION 7: FIGHT PLASTIC IN YOUR KITCHEN

You just got a new job. You are the bag police! Announce a zero tolerance plastic-bag policy. Make sure every member of your family has NO EXCUSE for using a plastic bag. Put canvas bags in the car, under the sink and always to hand, then charge each member of your family 10p for every plastic bag they use.

20 POINTS

Trade plastic scourers for coconut husk or metal ones, use cotton dishcloths instead of plastic ones and refill your washing-up liquid bottle at your local eco or plastic-free shop.

30 POINTS

Choose your favourite cereal. Find the biggest and smallest boxes of it that you can. Work out how many bowls of cereal each box contains and how many boxes of each size you'd need to fill 100 bowls.

10 POINTS

Make beeswax wraps with an adult. Find your brightest cotton fabric and paint it with beeswax (buy it online). If you are vegan, use plant-based wax. You can add pine resin to make the wraps sticky.

40 POINTS

TOTAL MISSION POINTS: 100

MISSION 8: FIGHT PLASTIC IN YOUR GARDEN

Use the compost you made in Mission 2. Put some compost into pots and plant some sunflower seeds. Watch them grow really tall!

20 POINTS

Cut a clear plastic bottle in half and fill the bottom with compost. Push three pea seeds around the bottle's edge. Water and leave on a window sill. You'll be able to see the seeds germinate and the seedlings grow. When they're big enough, plant them outside in a larger pot. Either cut and add the pea shoots to your salad or wait to eat the peas.

20 POINTS

Talk to your teacher about starting a gardening club or growing salad or veg in your classroom. Bring in leftover plastic pots, trays and containers and then take the veg home when it's big enough to eat.

20 POINTS

TOTAL MISSION POINTS: 60

MISSION 9: FIGHT PLASTIC IN YOUR BATHROOM

Try a toothbrush made of bamboo, one of the world's fastest-growing and most sustainable materials. When you have finished with it, you can put it in your compost.

20 POINTS

Try toothpaste that comes in a glass jar or in tablet form. It might not be what you are used to but it will work and is a fab way to fight plastic twice a day!

20 POINTS

Change your soap! Get rid of the squirty stuff and replace it with a bar of solid soap that comes wrapped in paper.

10 POINTS

Try out a solid shampoo bar and use solid soap instead of shower gel.

10 POINTS

At your local supermarket, try to find toilet paper that comes wrapped in paper.

10 POINTS

Look for cotton buds with paper sticks. Buy these instead.

10 POINTS

TOTAL MISSION POINTS: 80

MISSION 10: FIGHT PLASTIC IN YOUR LOO

Ask your teacher to organize a visit to your local sewage treatment plant. It might not sound like fun but it'll be VERY interesting.

100 POINTS

Count up the number of loos that you use regularly. Make a sign for each one that says: ONLY PEE, PAPER, PUKE AND POO DOWN THIS LOO – THANK YOU!

20 POINTS

If your family flushes anything down the loo that isn't one of the FOUR "P"s, ask if you can put a bin – with a lid – next to the loo, for everything else. These items can then go in the rubbish or be recycled.

20 POINTS

If your family uses wet wipes, make a notice for your loo reminding everyone not to flush them!

10 POINTS

TOTAL MISSION POINTS: 150

MISSION 11: FIGHT PLASTIC IN YOUR WARDROBE

Learn how to sew up holes in your old clothes.

10 POINTS

Separate your clothes that are made from man-made fibres from those made of natural fibres. Wash them less often.

10 POINTS

Catch microfibres in the washing machine with a specially designed bag or ball. Bin the fibres.

10 POINTS

Organize a clothes swap at school or at a club. Bring in the clothes you don't love any more and swap them for your friends' unloved clothes.

10 POINTS

Make yourself your very own **#2minutesuperhero** costume out of your old clothes.

20 POINTS

TOTAL MISSION POINTS: 60

MISSION 12: FIGHT PLASTIC ON THE PITCH, COURT, TRACK AND COURSE

Declare your sports events plastic-free. If you take snacks, go for homemade flapjacks or cakes, and ALWAYS remember to carry your reusable water bottle!

20 POINTS

Get your team to do a litter pick after every game. Take a bag and pick up any litter. Recycle what you can. You will look great and will be WINNING, whatever happens in the game.

30 POINTS

Grab a bag at lunchtime and go plogging around the playground!

30 POINTS

TOTAL MISSION POINTS: 80

MISSION 13: FIGHT PLASTIC ON YOUR DAYS OUT

Do a **#2minutebeachclean** and see what you find. Look for plastic bags, bottles, bottle tops, cotton-bud sticks, wet wipes and bits of fishing net. They are the most common items we find. But also look for Lego, toy soldiers, fishing lines and old flip-flops.

10 POINTS

Make it a plastic-free film night!

10 POINTS

Go to your favourite fast-food restaurant and test them to see if you can make your fast food a plastic-free affair. You can!

10 POINTS

TOTAL MISSION POINTS: 30

MISSION 14: FIGHT PLASTIC WITH YOUR POCKET MONEY

Stop spending your pocket money on one item that contains plastic. If it's sweets, go to a pick-and-mix instead. If it's toys, buy something that is plastic-free and you will keep.

20 POINTS

Ask your school to organize a bring-and-buy sale, where you and your friends can sell your unwanted books, toys and clothes – and earn money too!

40 POINTS

TOTAL MISSION POINTS: 60

MISSION 15: FIGHT PLASTIC IN YOUR CELEBRATIONS

Make presents for your family and wrap them in paper, newspaper or paper you have decorated yourself. Tie them up with string (sticky tape is plastic!).

30 POINTS

Make a paper chain to decorate your house. How long can you make it?

10 POINTS

Make a Halloween costume out of things you wear every day. Or borrow something silly. A scary hairstyle or face paints can transform an outfit into something really terrifying. Make it your mission to have a plastic-free Halloween.

20 POINTS

Make sure the chocolate you eat this Easter is not covered in plastic. Choose your eggs wisely!

10 POINTS

TOTAL MISSION POINTS: 70

MISSION 16: THE FIGHT-PLASTIC PARTY

Next time you have a birthday party or celebration, make it a FIGHT-PLASTIC PARTY! Plan carefully. Make your own decorations and cook up a party-food fiesta! Use the lists in this mission to help you.

150 POINTS

TOTAL MISSION POINTS: 150

BONUS MISSION: FIGHT PLASTIC WITH YOUR VOICE

Write a letter or an email to someone who is responsible for making decisions that affect your fight against plastic. It could be a Member of Parliament, a local councillor, a teacher or your headteacher. Tell them what worries you about plastic, what you need them to do and why. Go for it! Your voice matters.

100 POINTS

TOTAL MISSION POINTS: 100

WHAT KIND OF SUPERHERO ARE YOU?

Now you've completed the 2 minute missions, add up your points. What kind of #2minutesuperhero are you?

0-499 POINTS

You are my kind of superhero. You are getting there, putting in the effort, trying hard. And that's what matters. You have completed enough missions to start making a real difference. You care. You try to influence others. You are using your voice to make changes to your world.

Now is the time to make the most of your progress and do even more to save the ocean. So it's time to put on your cape and mask, go out into the world and do even more for Planet Earth. Everything you do makes a difference!

MISSION COMPLETE: You're a 3 ★ Superhero

500-999 POINTS

You have a whole superhero thing going on! You have completed most of the missions and that makes you a super-duper superhero. You have shown a real commitment to the ocean and a love of all things wild – the dolphins, whales and fish thank you.

What next? Complete the remaining missions and give the oceans one last push for their future. You can do it. You got this far by being a caring, plastic-fighting warrior! You can go the whole way. GO, YOU!

MISSION COMPLETE: You are a proper 4 ★ Superhero

1,000-1,500 POINTS

Oh my word! You are the Hero of the Superhero. How will you sleep at night, with all the praise I am about to give you? You have truly embraced the fight-plastic spirit and channelled your inner everyday superhero. Without a doubt, you have single-handedly saved dolphins, seals, whales and seabirds from plastic. Your work matters, and all your actions, combined with the actions of all the other superheroes out there, have made a real difference.

Top marks! Thank you and well done.

MISSION COMPLETE: You get the 5 ⭐ Superhero Award

INSERT YOUR PHOTO HERE

EVERYDAY SUPERHERO

What's your name?

What's your job?

What's your superpower?

How do you fight plastic?

What's your top tip?

What do you hate?

What do you love?

YOU

FIND OUT MORE ABOUT THE FIGHT AGAINST PLASTIC

Want to learn more? Excellent! Take a look at these:

CAMPAIGNS AND ACTIVISM

Kids Against Plastic: a charity set up by kids for kids
www.kidsagainstplastic.co.uk

Surfers Against Sewage: a community dedicated to the protection of the oceans, beaches and wildlife
www.sas.org.uk

Greenpeace: a global organization that defends the natural world and is campaigning to stop the flow of plastic into the ocean
www.greenpeace.org.uk/what-we-do/oceans/plastics

Keep Britain Tidy: join a clean-up with this environmental charity
www.keepbritaintidy.org

Marine Conservation Society: the UK's leading marine charity
www.mcsuk.org

RESOURCES

Less Plastic: find fantastic posters and infographics about plastic pollution
www.lessplastic.co.uk

Global Ocean: download activities, posters and leaflets
www.globalocean.org.uk/resources

World Oceans Day: get involved with this global celebration by planning an event
www.worldoceansday.org

The Wild Tribe Heroes: read stories about animals who find themselves in trouble in the ocean
www.wildtribeheroes.com

MORE ABOUT MARTIN

Hello. This is me. I am Martin Dorey. I'm a surfer, writer, beach lover and anti-plastic activist. I live near the sea in Cornwall with my partner, Lizzy, who is also known as Dr Seaweed. She's a gardener and botanist. My children, Maggie and Charlotte, live down the road from me with their dog Bob, a medium-sized pooch of unknown origin. They sometimes come beach-cleaning with me.

I have too many surfboards, a big camper van and a bike that I enjoy riding down muddy hills with Dr Seaweed. I like writing, camping, clean beaches, eating flapjacks and waking up to sunny days by the sea with the people I love the most.

MORE ABOUT THE #2MINUTEBEACHCLEAN

The **#2minutebeachclean** is a campaign that began many years ago. After discovering an area of my local beach knee-deep in plastic bottles, I vowed, there and then, that I would do something, anything, to make a difference.

I set up The Beach Clean Network in 2009 and then began using the **#2minutebeachclean** hashtag on social media in 2013. The idea is very simple: each time you go to the beach, you take 2 minutes to pick up beach litter, take a picture of it and then post it to social media to inspire others to do the same. In 2014, The Beach Clean Network set up 8 Beach Clean Stations around Cornwall that make it really easy for people to pick up litter at the beach. In 2019, there are over 500 litter-picking stations, with one of the most used in a school.

The **#2minutebeachclean** has now evolved into the **#2minutelitterpick** and the **#2minutestreetclean**, as well as the **#2minutesolution**. On social media, we've seen that our thousands of followers are fighting plastic every day by cleaning beaches, picking up litter from the streets where they live or making plastic-free choices. All I ask is that, having read this book, you continue to take 2 minutes out of your day to pick up litter, make a change or cut out plastic from your life. It might not seem like much, but when you add it to everyone else's efforts, it begins to make a big difference.

In 2019, The Beach Clean Network will become a charity: The 2 Minute Foundation.

Find out more: **www.beachclean.net**

With thanks to:

Lizzy

Daisy, Maria and all at Walker Books

Nicky, Dolly, Andrea, Adam, Alan, Tab, Jackie,
the **#2minutebeachclean** team
and the **#2minutebeachclean** family

Chris Hines

My superheroes: Neil Hembrow (KBT), Deb Rosser (ReFill South West), Rowena Bird (Lush), Rob Thompson (Ocean Recovery Project), Linda Thomas (Eco Design), Pete Cooper (The Crackington Crew) and the legendary Jim Scown (ex-RNLI)

Also: British Divers Marine Life Rescue, The Cornish Seal Sanctuary, Clive Symm, The Crackington Crew, Widemouth Task Force, The Plastic Movement, Surfers Against Sewage, Paddle Against Plastic, and all the amazing anti-plastic groups in the UK and beyond who are making a huge difference.